RAGDOLL CATS

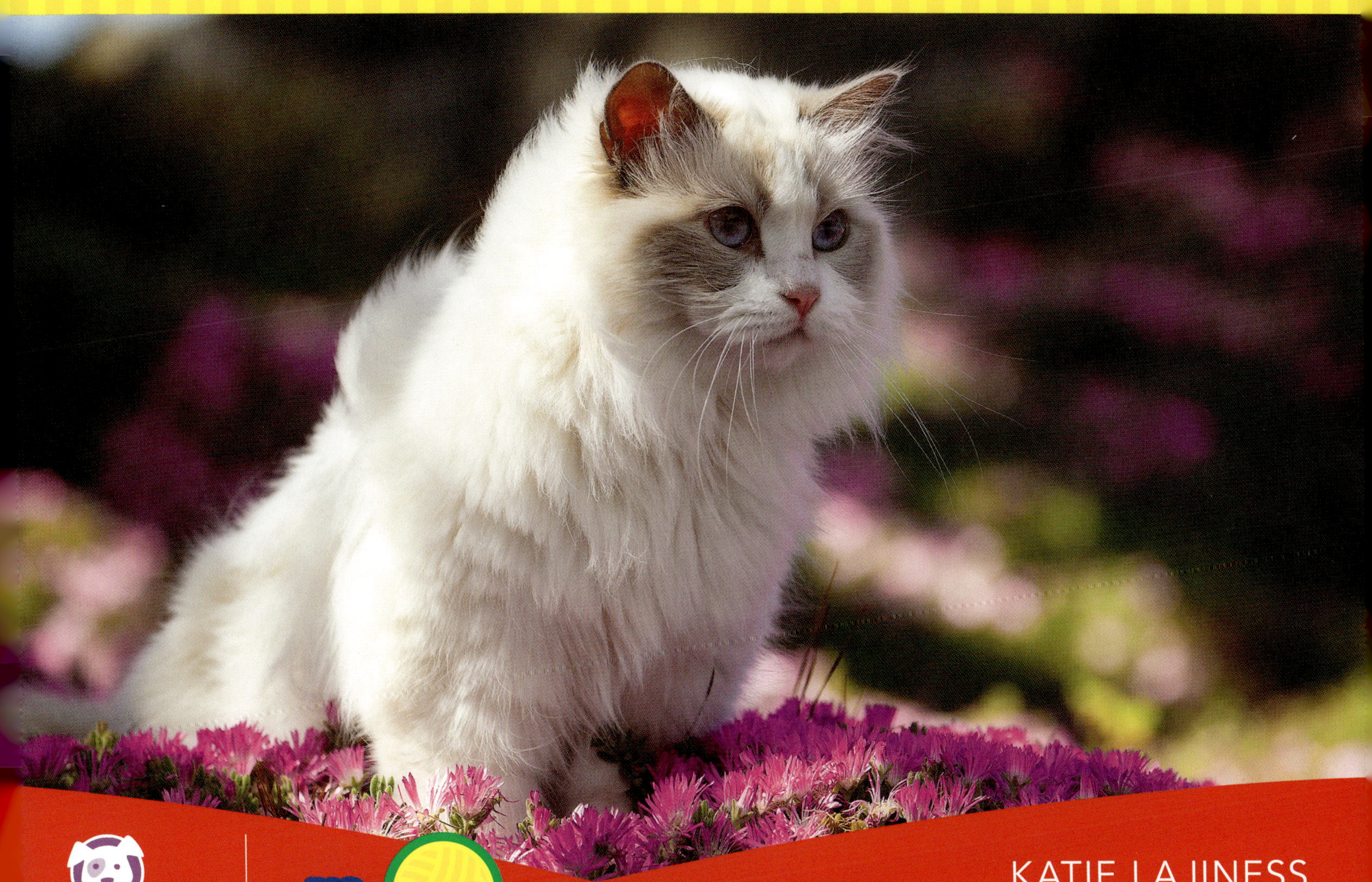

KATIE LAJINESS

Big Buddy Books
Imprint of Abdo Publishing
abdopublishing.com

BIG BUDDY CATS

abdopublishing.com

Published by Abdo Publishing, a division of ABDO, PO Box 398166, Minneapolis, Minnesota 55439.

Big Buddy Books™ is a trademark and logo of Abdo Publishing.

Printed in the United States of America, North Mankato, Minnesota.
092017
012018

THIS BOOK CONTAINS
RECYCLED MATERIALS

Cover Photo: Getty Images.
Interior Photos: Alamy Stock Photo (pp. 19, 23); Getty Images (pp. 5, 7, 9, 13, 15, 17, 21, 25, 27, 29, 30); Wang He/Stringer/Getty Images (p. 11).

Coordinating Series Editor: Tamara L. Britton
Contributing Editor: Jill Roesler
Graphic Design: Jenny Christensen

Publisher's Cataloging-in-Publication Data

Names: Lajiness, Katie, author.
Title: Ragdoll cats / by Katie Lajiness.
Description: Minneapolis, Minnesota : Abdo Publishing, 2018. | Series: Big buddy cats | Includes online resources and index.
Identifiers: LCCN 2017943924 | ISBN 9781532112027 (lib.bdg.) | ISBN 9781614799092 (ebook)
Subjects: LCSH: Ragdoll cat--Juvenile literature. | Cats--Juvenile literature.
Classification: DDC 636.83--dc23
LC record available at https://lccn.loc.gov/2017943924

CONTENTS

A POPULAR BREED

Cats are popular pets. About 35 percent of US households have a cat. And, Americans own more than 85 million!

Around the world, there are more than 40 **domestic cat breeds**. One of these is the ragdoll cat. Let's learn why the ragdoll is the second-most popular cat breed in the United States.

Cats enjoy sitting on perches. Being up high makes a cat feel secure.

THE CAT FAMILY

All cats belong to the **Felidae** family. There are 37 **species** in this family. **Domestic cats** are part of one species. Lions and other types of cats make up the others.

Did you know?

Humans and cats have lived together for at least 3,500 years.

Farmers first used domestic cats to help keep rats and mice out of their grain.

RAGDOLL CATS

Ragdoll cats did not develop in nature. Rather, **breeder** Ann Baker created the ragdoll in the early 1960s. She **bred** her **domestic cat** with a series of stray cats.

These beautiful cats went floppy when picked up! So, Baker called the new breed ragdoll.

The first ragdoll cats came from Riverside, California.

In 1971, Baker started a ragdoll cat association. She had strict rules about how to **breed** ragdolls. But some **breeders** did not agree with the rules.

Breeders Laura and Denny Dayton started their own group. Because of this, most cat **registries** began accepting the ragdoll. One of these is the **Cat Fanciers' Association**.

Today, many cat associations exist. The International Cat Association is one of the most popular.

WHAT THEY'RE LIKE

Ragdoll cats have sweet, friendly natures. They get along well with children and other pets.

Ragdolls are laid-back but very social animals. Like dogs, some greet guests at the door!

Ragdolls do not make much noise. They hardly ever meow, except when they want food!

COAT AND COLOR

Ragdolls are long-haired cats with silky fur. It is a pointed **breed**. So, its body is a lighter color than its face, legs, tail, and ears.

This breed has a double coat. The undercoat is covered with long, lightweight fur. The ragdoll's fur does not easily tangle like other long-haired breeds.

Cats in this breed can have four different coat patterns and six different colors.

SIZE

The ragdoll is a large cat. At four years old, ragdolls reach their full size and weight. Males weigh 15 to 20 pounds (7 to 9 kg). Females are somewhat smaller. They weigh ten to 15 pounds (5 to 7 kg).

This **breed** has an uncommon look. It has large paws and tufts of fur between its toes. A ragdoll cat has a long body with longer fur around its neck.

All ragdoll cats have blue, oval-shaped eyes. However, their eyes can be many shades of blue.

FEEDING

Healthy cat food includes beef, chicken, or fish. A good name-brand food will provide the **nutrients** a cat needs.

Cat food can be dry, semimoist, or canned. Food labels will show how much and how often to feed a cat.

As cats age, their bodies lose the ability to digest any type of milk.

CARE

Cats rarely need a bath to keep them clean. Instead, regular **grooming** helps prevent knotted fur. Brushing removes loose hair, so the cat won't swallow it when grooming itself. The balls of fur a cat might swallow are called hair balls.

Did you know?

A cat should have its ears checked often to avoid germs.

A cat should have its claws trimmed every ten to 14 days. A scratching post provides a spot for a cat to sharpen its claws. This way, it won't ruin any furniture.

Ragdoll cats need a good veterinarian. The vet can provide health exams and **vaccines**. He or she can also **spay** or **neuter** cats.

Kittens need to see the vet several times during their first few months. Adult cats should visit the vet once a year for a checkup.

Ragdolls love running water! They will play in water if given the chance.

Cats have an **instinct** to bury their waste. So, cats should use a **litter box**. Waste should be removed from the box daily.

A cat buries its waste to mark its area. If a cat goes outdoors, it will begin to do the same. A **microchip** can help bring a cat home if it gets lost.

Cats need a safe, warm place to sleep. The average cat sleeps about 16 hours a day.

KITTENS

A ragdoll mother is **pregnant** for 63 to 65 days. Then, she gives birth to a **litter** of about five kittens. For the first two weeks, kittens mostly eat and sleep.

All kittens are born blind and deaf. After two weeks, they can see and hear. But, they still stay close to their mother to feel warm and safe. At three weeks, the kittens begin taking their first steps.

During the 1990s, breeders used ragdolls to create a similar breed called RagaMuffins.

THINGS THEY NEED

Between 12 and 16 weeks old, ragdoll kittens are ready for **adoption**. Kittens like to be active. So, they need daily exercise. A ragdoll cat will be a loving companion for about 17 years.

Did you know?

Cats have whiskers on their cheeks, chins, eyebrows, ears, and front legs.

Cats enjoy sitting in small spaces, such as buckets or boxes.

GLOSSARY

adoption the process of taking responsibility for a pet.

breed a group of animals sharing the same appearance and features. To breed is to produce animals by mating.

breeder someone who breeds animals.

Cat Fanciers' Association established in 1906, it is the world's largest registry for pedigreed cats.

domestic cats tame cats that make great pets.

Felidae the scientific Latin name for the cat family. Members of this family are called felines. They include domestic cats, lions, tigers, lynx, and cheetahs.

groom to clean and care for.

instinct a way of behaving, thinking or feeling that is not learned, but natural.

litter all of the kittens born at one time to a mother cat.

litter box a place for house cats to leave their waste.

microchip an electronic circuit placed under an animal's skin. A microchip contains identifying information that can be read by a scanner.

neuter (NOO-tuhr) to remove a male animal's reproductive glands.

nutrient (NOO-tree-uhnt) something found in food that living beings take in to live and grow.

pregnant having one or more babies growing inside the body.

registry a place where official records are kept.

spay to remove a female animal's reproductive organs.

species (SPEE-sheez) living things that are very much alike.

vaccine (vak-SEEN) a shot given to prevent illness or disease.

ONLINE RESOURCES

Booklinks
NONFICTION NETWORK
FREE! ONLINE NONFICTION RESOURCES

To learn more about ragdoll cats, visit **abdobooklinks.com**. These links are routinely monitored and updated to provide the most current information available.

INDEX